MORE
Sunshine
on the
Soapsuds

Beneth Peters Jones

BOB JONES UNIVERSITY PRESS
GREENVILLE, SOUTH CAROLINA 29614

More Sunshine on the Soapsuds
by Beneth Peters Jones

© 1983 Bob Jones University Press
Greenville, South Carolina 29614

A compilation of "Sunshine on the Soapsuds" articles, taken from
FAITH for the Family, 1976-1982

ISBN 0-89084-192-6

Printed in the United States of America

For Bobby and Stephen,
who lend both bubbles and
sunshine to our home

Contents

Acknowledgements
Introduction
1 Chickens 1
2 Love and Giving 5
3 Growing Up 9
4 Whisperings 12
5 Bugs 16
6 Pilgrim's Daily 20
7 Cutting the Threads 24
8 Mathematics 28
9 Thing-a-ma-jigs 32
10 Behind the Wheel 36
11 Blind 40
12 Term Merchants 44
13 Surprise Ending 48
14 What's in a Name 51
15 Daffodils 54
16 Relative Positions 57
17 Words of Wisdom 62
18 Spilled Milk 67
19 Point of View 71
20 Traces of Salt 75
21 Slip-ups 79
22 Time Tested 82
23 Preserves 86
24 The Manx 90
25 A Missing String 95

Acknowledgements

Having produced the original articles herein via pressure, pain, and perspiration, I was delighted to turn them over to the supremely capable hands of Julia Hansen, editor, Jim Hargis, artist, and the faithful, effective staff of *FAITH for the Family* for this publication.

Introduction

Christian womanhood. What a rainbow expanse lies between its emergence in girlhood and its ending in death! That lovely rainbow grew most strongly evident to me while, in Washington State my mother lay dying, and here in South Carolina my daughter moved forward out of childhood.

Though we may long for a full experiencing of that rainbow, so often it eludes us. Why? There are, I believe, several reasons for our lives being less colorful and radiant than we and God would have them be. First, we seek for the wrong colors: we allow ourselves to be misdirected into the world's striving for the solids; the louds. Their gaudiness lures us from the gentler hues of God's design; their boldness leaves us, ultimately, drained and pale in our Christian testimony.

Second, we seek for solidity—yet the very essence of a rainbow is its breathtaking lack of substance and its brevity. Why do we try to hold on to "now" when it is gone before we can even speak the word itself? Why seek to establish an unchanging identity, state, pursuit, or possession when all of life is made up of imperceptible blendings upon the pallette of time?

Third, we try to *will* the color of Christian testimony into our lives—dictating to God our own desires and restrictions for service. Our hearts say, "I'll be glad to have lavender, Lord, but certainly *not* green!" And our willfulness or reluctance results in our Heavenly Father's withholding from us the hues He would have so beautifully used for His own glory.

What then *is* the rainbow of a Christian woman's testimony? It is comprised of *delicate* colors—femininity, submissiveness, servanthood, a meek and quiet spirit. It is *varied*—changing subtly or startlingly from edge to edge, with each pigment lovely in itself but also lovely in its coordination with all the others. And finally, the rainbow of Christian womanhood can only appear as *God Himself* paints it. Ours are only the indiscernible droplets of moisture suspended by the power of His love, content to catch and reflect the lightening, warming, coloring radiance of His sufficiency across the entire length and width of our fleeting existence.

My sincere prayer is that this second collection of "Sunshine on the Soapsuds" articles will direct the heart of each reader to a closer contemplation of the Sun of Righteousness and into the greater dedication of life that will allow Him to create in and through you a unique, effective rainbow of testimony.

Beneth Peters Jones
Hebrews 12:2

1
Chickens

It's very difficult for me to watch, unmoved, a truck going down the highway loaded with short, slatted crates stacked high to accommodate a cargo of chickens on their way to market. Viewing chickens as drumsticks and wishbones is a relatively recent development for me. Throughout childhood and adolescence they were much more—they were personalities.

Almost everywhere we lived, we had a full complement of chickens in the backyard. We raised them—not for commercial purposes, but because Daddy loved them. Consequently, we children developed—if not his love—at least some of his interest in chickens.

Almost without exception, our small flocks were red and white—specifically, the breeds known as Rhode Island Reds and Rhode Island

Whites. Daddy's delight was in breeding to
develop fine characteristics in the birds: full,
rosy combs and wattles, broad breasts, and
heavy bodies. The mere thought of allowing
leghorn-like traits to appear was heresy. He
dismissed the whole idea of "dumb, scrawny
leghorns" with an eloquent snort. Any fowl, be
it cockerel or pullet, that had the misfortune of
being narrowly constructed was soon invited to
supper—as the main course.

Watching chickens go from down to decrepi-
tude provided some insights denied city
children. No two of our chickens were alike.
Daddy, of course, intimately knew the traits
of each. But even we kids recognized and
accepted the fact that the feathered denizens
of our backyard were individuals. There was
the copper-hued patriarch whose strut became
more pathetic each year as his tail feathers
dropped off and his crow weakened and
cracked. But from Daddy's point of view, his
privileged position was clear; and that position
was guarded with downright violence. Just let a
young rooster cock his head, utter a quarreling
rattle, and move menacingly toward the totter-
ing monarch and he'd be knocked across the
yard by whatever lay nearest my dad's throwing
arm. That old rooster and Daddy spent many
an hour talking to each other. Daddy would put
him on his lap or on an apple box and pet and

praise him; the rooster would voice his appreciation of the gentle attention. The demise of that grand old fellow brought palpable gloom to the Peters household.

I learned something of Daddy's love for individual chickens by adopting as my own a half-bantam chick. As soon as his scandalous ancestry became evident, my father was bent on eliminating from his flock what he considered a living insult to poultrydom. But for some strange reason that gawky, multi-colored chick became the object of my childish championship. Then, having successfully rescued him from the chopping block, I proceeded to concentrate upon his adoption, amid warnings to "keep him away from my *good* chickens!" I settled upon "Ebenezer" as a suitably elegant name. As the year progressed, I think even Daddy was surprised by the strong pet-owner tie which formed. Ebenezer preferred my company to that of his fellows and would race to me when called. "That runt," as my dad termed him, gave his featherclad heart to me alone. Likewise, he was to be the only object of my personal affection in all of chickendom. When Daddy had to kill Ebenezer because he'd contracted cancer, I was sure my heart would never mend.

These and other memories go through my mind when a chicken truck rolls past. And now—a lesson from *chickens?* Yes. My distress over the helpless feathered creatures being carted to destruction reminds me of a far greater reason for distress: the numberless souls all around us who are on the devil's truck, so to speak, bound for a fate incomparably worse than physical destruction. Chickens are necessarily expendable. Their worth can be counted in pennies. But the unsaved human beings around us are worth so much that God's own Son died to save them. How dare we consider their indescribably horrible plight to be of small consequence!

2
Love and Giving

Our younger son gave me a gift last fall—a gift he had constructed with much humming and hammering, privacy and painting. Finally, in the evening, I was allowed to see it: a black, roughly square framework decorated with yellow and red swirls of poster paint. Grinning from ear to ear, Stephen said, "I made it for you, Mama. I don't know what it is. But I made it all by myself." The carpentry and artwork were impressive for a seven-year-old's efforts, and the love that had prompted the giving studded the offering with invisible diamonds.

For a day or so the undesignated gift occupied a portion of the kitchen table. But knowing that true appreciation is only shown by utilization, I assigned a task to the gift: umbrella rack for the garage.

This gift and numberless others like it roll the years away and show me the country child who almost daily returned from her woodland wanderings with hands full of gifts for her mother. The woods were never selfish in their offerings; nor could I be niggardly in passing them along to Mother. I don't remember calling to her as I ran toward the house, but I must have: for memory paints her standing in the open doorway, an apron over her housedress, watching my galloping approach. Nor do I recall the procession of gifts which passed from my hands to hers, except for one—a bouquet gathered at creekside.

The leaves were smooth and shiny, the blossom an intriguing waxy cluster of bulbous entities, and the odor was unlike anything I'd ever experienced before. Delighted with this botanical treasure, my five-year-old hands went immediately to work and kept at it until I'd gathered an impressively large bouquet. Charging up the hill, I bestowed the flowers upon my mother. An unusual tightness in her vocal tone gave the first clue that something was amiss. Looking up at her face as she bent over me, I verified the suspicion. There was a smile on her lips, but it looked a trifle forced. And she was backing ever so slowly away from me, holding my bouquet, but holding it as far from her as possible. Then she started to laugh. Mom's laugh wasn't something you just listened to: it caught you and caused you to join its lilt. But I couldn't understand why we were laughing. Then between chuckles she explained: "Benne, we'll have to keep this bouquet outside. It can't come in the house, Honey."

"But why not, Mom?"

"Because this is skunk cabbage! Here— smell." She squeezed one of the waxy blossoms, and the pungent odor stung my nostrils.

"Ugh. It *does* smell awful!" Taking the bouquet, I headed shedward for a can to serve as outdoor flower container. My mother's voice followed my trek: "Thank you for the present, Honey! What a nice little girl you are to pick all those flowers and bring them to me! We'll enjoy looking out at them through the window."

Skunk cabbage. A garage umbrella rack. So it goes from generation to generation: a child demonstrates love for the parent by bringing gifts. Gifts awkward, nondescript, odiferous, mangled; but gifts nonetheless. And because of the adoring love which prompts the giving, their worth outstrips material evaluation.

Love and giving: an intertwining, inseparable reality. It's easy to see their relationship in the natural sense, but it is repeatedly denied in the spiritual. We try to make our love for Jesus Christ a separate entity to be placed at Point A in our lives. Then somewhere far down the line, perhaps at about Point G, we place giving. By this dichotomy we try to make our giving—of self, service, and separation—an elective consideration. But our attempt contradicts the clear indication in God's Word that love and giving are mutually dependent: giving is empty apart from love; and love is a sham when it doesn't move us to give.

3
Growing Up

Today, quietly and without fanfare, we reached a landmark at our house. It was simply a girl's voice behind me, as I scoured the bathroom floor on hands and knees, saying, "Mom, is it okay if I give my dolls and doll clothes to someone? They're in my way."

Grateful to be facing the floor, I responded with what I hoped was an emotionally unrevealing "Well, yes, if that's what you want to do." And that initial reaction was admirably followed up with calm advice on packing the dolls. And yet the moment was a family landmark. Now, as the fireplace burns low in a sleeping house, I can look back with an emotional honesty necessarily denied at the time. And the tears come; for today my little girl has taken a giant step away from childhood toward adulthood.

While we worked together packing the dolls

away, temptation was strong to pause over each one, cherishing photo-sharp memories associated with it. There was the ruffle-skirted doll from Spain which had fascinated a five-year-old, inspiring her to a period of flowers in the hair. And the baby doll whose bedraggled locks shouted of numberless scrub-and-comb sessions by chubby hands. Or the less cuddly number which brought squeals of delight by its walking ability. Or the battered lifesize doll baby whose chubby form had worn its owner's outgrown baby clothes.

The nostalgia was mine alone; Roxane was delighted to be moving the "babyish" items out of her room. And in view of her obvious relief and sense of advancement, a revelation of my melancholy would have had a dampening effect. So, instead, resolutely trying to share her enthusiasm, I turned away from the days of rufflereared pink tights, bouffant baby dresses, size 2 patent leather shoes, hair ribbons, and ruffled socks. Those things must forever be put away in the golden locket of memory which hangs at the heart of every mother. Only at quiet, lonely moments can the locket be opened and the sweet-scented reminiscences brought out to enjoy.

From that unforgettable landmark moment, my daughter and I have been facing forward. Together we are enjoying the fleeting girl-woman interlude with its growth spurt, emotional roller coaster, behavioral inconsistencies, personality and character solidification, and appearance alterations. Remembering the importance of my mother's warm solidity in my own pubescence, I'm seeking by the Lord's help to contribute a like encouragement for Roxane's. And, rather than finding this transitional period agony, we're both finding it, for the most part, exciting and fun. Walking in cooperative understanding now is also giving us added anticipation of even greater enjoyment in the future when the metabolic storms will subside and the comparative calm of maturity sweep in.

Turning point, yes. But cause for lingering sadness? No. If my daughter were not to put away her dolls and make maturational advancement, there would be cause for agonizing sorrow. Growth is not without its pain; yet that growth is a desired evidence of normality. Roxane's gleeful dash toward adulthood poses a question for my heart: In my Christian life have I been willing and eager to put away the childish interests acceptable in the infantile but regrettable in the mature? May it be so, dear Lord!

4
Whisperings

It was a little boy's prayer in family devotions for his grandmother far away: "Dear Jesus, please let Grandma hear You whispering to her while she's lying there in a coma." Thus childish lips raised a request cross-stitched with simplicity, embroidered with emotional eloquence, while adult petitioners knelt mutely by.

There are times of testing in the life of every Christian when some burden weighs so heavily that the crushed heart loses even its knowledge of how to frame its pleadings with its Lord. A soul torn with sorrow, a mind distracted by the sudden plunge into shadow, a body weary from emotional draining—all these combine to make the petitionary heart a silent thing; knees will bend and head will bow, but the agonized spirit can only frame an incomplete "Oh, dear Lord, please ..." Is that prayer? Indeed—prayer of the most intense kind: in it we know the reality of that verse, "Likewise the Spirit also helpeth our infirmities: for we know not what we should pray for as we ought: but the Spirit itself maketh intercession for us with groanings which cannot be uttered." Oh, blessed comfort! Some trials must necessarily silence us, that we may learn the reality of God's still small voice and the explicitness of the Holy Spirit's intercession.

Towering sorrow and overwhelming loss shrink us by their magnitude, stripping from us all sense of direction. Within this shrivelled shell can be found no guidepost of reason, no road-map of impulse. Only the compass of faith abides constant.

To look at the source of our sorrow gives no helpful cue. This loved one lying sheeted and still a nation's breadth away, what would she want for herself in these days, if she could say? Would she urge prayer for her injury-broken body's return to earthly activity, if such a return might mean lingering paralysis? For her mind working in fitful, unpredictable snatches, then drifting away with a sigh: should we ask that it be restored to control of a body no longer recognizable as its diamond-jubileed, chubby dwelling? What of her heart glimpsed through hurt-puzzled eyes searching a daughter's face and yearning unsuccessfully upward from the turgid depths of coma: should we pray for return to consciousness, when that consciousness could bring greater hurt?

Turn then to us—the helpless waiters by her bed: still no steady directional beam can be discerned. Should our hearts petition the Lord's mercy, His love, in restoration of this beloved mother and wife? Can we acceptably plead our continued need for her love, her laughter, her listening, her lighted life? Or ought we to simply ask for her painless passing through to the other side of the dark valley wherein she wanders?

The soul's weary groping through emotion's storms becomes a scribbled sigh:

Arms of comfort, hold her warmly,
She whose mother arms held me.
We who cherish her most dearly
Can no love compare with Thee.

Arms of mercy, hold her closely,
Nearer now than e'er before.
Sheeted white and silent queerly,
Far she drifts beyond our shore.

Arms of love, hold her supremely,
Treasured as Thy blood-bought child.
Poor of earth, of Heaven queenly,
Jew'lled by trust in Saviour mild.

Arms of power, hold her surely,
Weakened she by hurt and age.
We who wait must trust Thee wholly;
To Thy will our hearts engage.

The days of painful learning move slowly onward; lips continue mutely moving, claiming the Holy Spirit's intermediary verbalization. And her for whom we pray and weep? "Dear Jesus, please let Grandma hear You whispering to her while she's lying there in a coma." Amen, my son; oh, amen!

5
Bugs

Just as I'm about to draw a breath of relief at nearing the successful end of my daughter's junior high school education, I've been hit with the realization that, without so much as a decent pause, our elder son will move into that elite and demanding educational way station. Having survived the bug collection requirement once, I'm none too eager for a second go-round.

Helping Roxane collect bugs went against everything I'd ever known or practiced. Heretofore, I'd done my part in maintaining a reasonable human/insect balance by hastily dispatching anything buggy. But the collection changed all that. Strange as it seemed, we began looking for bugs, and that meant changed actions and reactions. Shiver-grown goose bumps gave place to anticipatory prickles. Whether the setting were home, yard, or countryside, we kept a sharp eye open for creepy-crawlers which could qualify as collectibles. Upon sighting a likely candidate, we initiated pursuit, oblivious to either ungainly posture requirements or unattractive hunting grounds.

Lacking sophisticated insect nets, we employed jars; and as the bug collection grew, my jar collection dwindled. In spite of advertised dishwasher sterilization capacities, any jar that had housed a candidate for collection automatically forfeited any further domestic use.

Catching the critter was only the beginning. A relatively delicate demise had then to be undertaken (no pun intended). The first execution rendered with scientific acceptability confirmed my preference for the old quick squish method. Nor will impaling the specimen on a straight pin win high marks as my favorite pastime. However, the finished collection, handsome in its size-and-type mounting, was of genuine satisfaction.

Between pursuit and display lay many hours of identification. In that book-bound activity I became aware of myriad fascinating details which make me wonder how I survived without them:

—Whereas "ladybug" had seemed an adequate term for the gentle little insects

I'd urged to "fly away home," I'm now burdened with the knowledge that I should by rights admonish either a *Coccinella novemnotato* or a *Hippodamia convergens* to dash in the direction of its domicile.

—The squishing reflex may suffer an interruptive pause from now on as I wonder whether the doomed *Dermaptera* be male or female. (Surely, however, the answer to that is only of interest to another earwig!)

—Unscientific, stomping pursuit of a cockroach can henceforth be lent added color by a gutteralized pronunciation of its scientific name, *Blatella germanica.*

—In harking back to a nasty sting by a bumble bee when I was knee high to a *Melanoplus mexicanus,* I feel sure the wound would have been greater had I recognized my attacker as a *Bombus speciosus.*

—A blush rises at remembering the two or three specimens whose little selves were labelled only "unidentified." Who knows what multi-syllabic nomenclature they should rightly bear!

Actually, though the collection made for moments both funny and squeamish, it has also made for fascination. Such minute creatures—yet what accuracy and delicacy can be seen in their construction; what unique equipages given by their Creator; what incredible rainbow colors emblazoned on bodies and wings!

Discovering the miniature world lying virtually underfoot has made me ponder: how many other marvels do I miss every day? Do I overlook the exotic by relying on the familiar? Do I circumnavigate the rare in pursuing the ordinary? We who know earth's Creator through saving faith in His Son should examine and exult in the intricate works of our Father's hand, any one of which can drive us to exclaim, "Be Thou exalted, O God, above the heavens: and Thy glory above all the earth" (Psalm 108:5).

6
Pilgrim's Daily

Until last fall, a newspaper was something that conveniently appeared on the doorstep at a more-or-less regular time each day. Perusal was followed by relegation to more physical services like protecting the kitchen floor from spattering grease or starting a fire in the fireplace. Nice. Simple. But not any more. As of October last, I became—howbeit reluctantly—Mother to a Newspaper Carrier. Looking at the assignment from the perspective of ignorance gave me qualms; those quivers would have been major quakes had I known in October what I know in April!

The appellation "Mother of a Newspaper Carrier" would more accurately translate "Newspaper Carrier." Bobby began delivering papers on October 1. Before two weeks had elapsed, he hurled himself at a soccer ball and collided with a goal post. Result: six stitches, two crutches, and 32 temporarily carrier-less newspapers. Because the route must be run in late afternoon, the carrier's male parent claimed exemption on the grounds of conflicting duties. Such exemption did not apply, however, to the female parent. So, housework deferred and younger son enlisted, I entered the world of newspaper delivery. It contains unique terrain.

The mountains of Delivery Domain are made of the papers themselves. According to the route supervisor's original sales pitch, the printed offerings would arrive at the pick-up point near 3:30 each afternoon. The first day's experience made me wonder what kind of measuring device was used to chart "near." Even after all these months I'm still wondering! But uncertain pick-up times were only gently-rolling landscape compared with what lay beyond. When finally "ready" for pick-up, the papers resisted the prescribed carrier action with several cunning maneuvers: they challenged folding attempts by either (a) their monstrous bulk or (b) their obviously pre-arranged agreement to self destruct. If defeated there in the foothilly problems, the papers rose to the rocks of obstinacy, where they fought bike basket confinement. Folded or flat, the load never really fit. The only solution was to stick the overflow into every available extrabasketal notch, thereby creating a porcu-bike. Still the problems built higher, until they reached alpine heights of sheer obnoxious cussedness as the papers shifted their weight ever so sneakily at moments of precarious balance, causing heart stoppages for both the basket-laden biker and for his mother puffingly peddling a rear guard position.

The final Everest towered when the papers were thrown—for in spite of every human victory up to that point, the newspapers perversely claimed triumph by breaking their rubber band bindings to demonstrate disintegrative flight, by diving into the only wet spot on an otherwise dry lawn, or by grabbing an arboreal roost.

Newspaperdom was not exclusively made of mountains, of course. It also abounded with valleys—the customers. The boggy glens were those who played musical subscriptions, taking the paper two days, then cancelling, only to call in a renewal the following week. The shale shallows were those who considered the newspaper a favorite lapdog to be carefully placed (*not* thrown) at the door (*not* on the lawn) by a certain time (*late* today, eh?). The gullies were the nonpayers and the attempted nonpayers. They took several forms: (a) peeking through blinds to silently watch the paper carrier fruitlessly wear out a finger on the doorbell; (b) going off for a season-long vacation without notifying the carrier, though already owing for two months' deliveries; (c) establishing a scheme to avoid having any family member at home other than between midnight and 2 a.m. Relieving the dent-dotted terrain, however, were the sunny vales of friendly subscribers who "adopted" the carrier (or his gasping replacement).

The plains of Delivery Land were the natural and mechanical hazards: nearly-vertical hills which made bike and carrier alike groan in agony; drenching rains that began halfway through the route; dogs that silently threatened or snarlingly charged; tree branches dedicated to carrier impalement; rush hour traffic bent upon cyclist annihilation. Thus route's end felt roughly equivalent to a Sahara survival.

All this—and more—goes into newpaper delivery. Demands and distractions notwithstanding, the news reaches its destination. God's Good News is likewise intended for delivery, and each of us believers is entered in God's records as a carrier. I wonder what kind of notations are being made as to our courage, dedication, and effectiveness.

7
Cutting the Threads

The literal sounds accompanying the chore were few and gentle: a creaking ironing board, a gliding iron, and the *whoosh* of escaping steam. The imagined sound was singular and distinct: my mother's voice in its well-remembered phrase, "Cut your threads, Honey, cut your threads!" Motivating her voice was the iron's collision with long, tangled threads in newly sewn seams.

No matter how simple the lesson, learning is not always easy. Mother had tried vainly to drill this principle into my head from the first time I'd sat down at a sewing machine: when making anything, a seamstress should always remember to *cut her threads* after tying off a line of stitching.

"Cut your threads." So many strands are involved in a life! Strong, useful threads go into joining seams and tailoring pieces for character and personality formation—threads of family, environment, spiritual atmosphere, etc. Yet each of those constructive processes, when finished, leaves threads of entanglement unless the strands are tied off and cut.

Childhood's stitchings were carefree and amusing. But they ended long ago. To turn from the responsibilities of maturity with backward-yearning eyes is profitless extension of threads. Neither the seam once finished nor the tuck once taken can be altered upon the fabric of life. Adulthood holds new, more important tasks: challenges of intricate fitting and finishing. An attempt to take up yesterday's threads will only clog today's machinery.

I know a woman whose chronological age is in the thirties; but psychologically she's in her eighties, because she has never cut the threads. To be in her presence five minutes is to hear her bring up some incident of childhood, recounting it with a relish which reveals a backward yearning. This young woman's emotional mechanism is stuck in "reverse," and she's entangled in childhood's threads. This subtle form of escapism is regrettable; her fascination with the past zigzags by the joys of the present. Where there should be rejoicing in love of husband, warmth of home, and fun of children, there is sighing for pampering of parents, prestige of heritage, and ease of girlhood.

The threads of my own life are more deli-cately formed: no cords of yearning for return to heedless childhood days these, but rather gossamer threads of reliance on maternal wisdom and warmth.

My marriage to a southerner scissored physical closeness with my western mother, yet it simultaneously bonded our hearts. Comfort, understanding, and encouragement have pulsed steadily through living connectives. Thereby, though finished with her major structural con-tribution to my life, Mother continued to enrich my spirit with delicate lace edging.

Today, maternal weaving hands have lain still for more than a year and slack threads slip through cold fingers to dangle loosely from abruptly ended lace. Cutting those threads brings searing pain; yet severed they must be, for their usefulness is over, their precious embellishment ended. To leave them forever attached from living to dead would be to abuse the loveliness of the past and to betray the beauty of the future.

Through falling tears, refracted light from eternity makes the time-stained threads transparent, revealing the blessed words of Scripture,

"If in this life only we have hope in Christ, we are of all men most miserable. But now

is Christ risen from the dead, and become
the firstfruits of them that slept."

Oh, glorious day when strands of life and
love will be spun of everlasting gold! Until then,
beloved Mother, enabled by the Lord and motivated by your words, I do what must be done:
cut the threads . . . cut the threads!

8
Mathematics

"Hold on, old girl—you'll make it through. Come on, grit your teeth; it can't really be endless!" Who said that? Me. What "can't really be endless"? The school year. Why the big deal, the desperate tone? Because!

When I was a student myself, homework didn't hold the horrors it does now. In fact, I remember really enjoying my studies. Maybe for that very reason I feel that now it's someone else's turn. After all, one eighteen-year-long stint of studies is enough for one person, right?

Wrong—at least for this mother of grade-schoolers. Having staggered squinty-eyed through two elementary-age offspring, my stagger is becoming a limp with my third.

"Homework" actually translates better as

"arithmetic," and automatic conjugation of the verb "to hate" responds to that translation. Yet, inevitably, it's math which daily comes home in Stephen's book bag. A high point of my life was the day on which I took leave of mathematical studies back in high school; evidently the leave was not permanent!

Little patience enters any given homework session; none comes out. It dissolves on Problem # 43, when the scholar's fifteenth solution to 7-times-9 is still incorrect. But, I ask you, what patience would withstand the constant dripping of acids like the following:

Someone changed things while I wasn't looking. I'm sure my math book didn't contain all those charts with arrows, squares, circles, and shadings. New terms have sneaked in, too, or are appearing earlier. What is a "prime number"? And why are they talking about geometry in third grade? Anyway, in order to help solve the problems, I'm forced to plow through the "perfectly clear" diagram/explanations. Ideally, I suppose, I should glean from those pictured presentations the same thing the teacher does. But my Number Three Child insists that I don't; he stubbornly holds to the ridiculous theory that I'm not having him do the problem the way the teacher did. Then, in spite of my herculean efforts, he gloomily reports poor grades on his homework!

There is a ray of hope, however; as did the other two children before him, this one will surely reach that blissful point where he learns: 1) mathematical principles and practice are conquerable and 2) Mother's iron-willed assistance is expendable.

In subsequent years, of course, I take great (wondering!) pride in the children's smoothly sailing mathematical ship, with some of the pleasure coming from knowing the near-fatal shoals of homework-helping lie behind.

In my thoughts of dread before and self-flagellation after such sessions, I've dwelt on their applicability to things of the spirit. There are many experiences in life which are less than enjoyable. But just as surely as an earthly school teacher has the pupil's advancement as the ultimate goal of assignments, so does the Heavenly Father assign those lessons without which our spiritual knowledge remains infantile. Moreover, God's "homework assignments" for us are, in a sense, mathematical, since they are intended to do one or more of the following:

add to our spiritual depth
multiply our outreach
find the *square root* of our strength
subtract the dross from our lives,
and *divide* our burdens as we cast them
upon the Lord.

May we who joyously love the Lord in the "recess" periods of earth's school days be just as confident, joyful, and trusting in the times of our hardest "homework assignments."

9
Thing-a-ma-jigs

Recent years have brought a clumsy bird of reality to perch upon my shoulder croaking hoarsely in my ear, "*Look at you*—you're a *pack rat!*" That croak becomes a screech at housecleaning time. Any *one* drawer in our house can yield the most amazing assortment of items! Originally intended to hold, say, trading stamps and cents-off coupons, it tirelessly collects shoelaces, chopsticks, electrical fuses, scissors, gum, address cards, and numberless other items of sundry size, shape, and use.

How do all those things get in that drawer in the first place? I put them there, of course. Why? Just because. It all starts as I stand in a room holding one or more homeless items. Basically, the decision is to "keep it or dump it"—but dumping seems so *final*. On the other hand, that empty spool could possibly be needed (or at least used) some day . . . so it ends up being tossed into the nearest drawer to wait patiently for its non-materializing "someday."

The main lack in me at such moments of decision, doubtless, is that of organization. I realize that the ideal is "a place for everything, and everything in its place." Nice ideal—and I really *do* work consistently in that general direction; but *how* does one organize for the preservation and use of thing-a-ma-jigs? Having never arrived at a satisfactory answer to that question, I've never succeeded in finding or making the appropriate place for such category-defying objects.

There is a second part to this confession, as well. No matter how smart I manage to be on put-away day, tucking all sorts of interesting bits, pieces, knobs, and nadgets away hither and yon, my brilliancy evaporates—POOF!—the moment I *need* a bit, piece, knob, or nadget. Since they've been stuck in various undesignated, unorganized nooks and crannies all over the house, there is no earthly way for me to dredge up from memory which nook or what cranny was made the repository for the needed item.

Once a year or so I purge the house of the various saved goodies, and as they're pitched one by one over a shoulder into the trash, I

wonder *why* in the world, even in my wildest
moment, I'd ever thought there could be a
future use for *that* thing! Among my more
brilliant rat-packings have appeared the likes of:
2 1/3 inches of bright red ball fringe; 97 de-
tipped hairpins; 32 rusty paper clips; 521 non-
writing ballpoint pens; 5 color-bled scarves; 16
reels of recording tape (we have *never* owned a
reel-to-reel recorder!); 24 empty, lidless station-
ery boxes; and 13 metal shelf-adjustment clips
(of *course* I don't remember where the shelves
were, or when!). With such weighty evidence
against me, indictment as a veteran packrat
is certain.

The even more unpleasant truth is that my
squirreling doesn't limit itself to physical things.
It seems the pieces of information that lodge
most firmly in my brain for instant recall are
those *really* handy telephone numbers from
teenage years; a line of poetry apropos of nothing; a bit of information about the pigment-
mixing technique of an obscure 14th-century
Italian painter; a detail of costume development
which appeared in 1734; or the formula for
solving a high school geometry problem. Even
unconsciously my rodent tendencies have been
at work!

Because unused and unusables fill the
drawers of my house, the items that should be
therein have to be shuttled elsewhere; some-

times the really worthwhile materials are left homeless for years. The same is true, I'm afraid, of my mental and spiritual filing system. Trivia often triumphs, dislodging the really important items. For example, I carefully hoard hurts (real or imagined), preconceptions, and various lengths and shades of fears to such an extent that the drawers and shelves of my heart fairly groan at the load. Yet those things I *should* count precious and worthy of preservation are discarded carelessly here and there, coming to hand either unbidden or at oddly inappropriate moments, or reluctantly after long and hard search. Hence the groping for Scripture verses that I "sort of" know; the searching for forgiveness toward some person who long ago gave a wound to my spirit; the ruffling through sheaves of paper for a blank piece upon which to write a truly fresh impression; the scrambling for the exquisite ribbon of courage cherished from a spiritual victory.

Have patience yet, dear Lord! And as I learn to rightly sort, discard, and organize in my home, wilt Thou teach me to do so in my heart!

10
Behind the Wheel

"What did I ever do to deserve this?" That's a question that runs through my mind with great frequency these days—every time I get into our car, in fact—because "this" refers to my responsibility of training a budding driver! The hair-silvering experience may well prove beyond my survival capabilities.

Until December twelfth of the past year, I ignored, with comparative success, the rapid growth rate of our three children. Although hugging calls for more fully extended arms and kissing for less and less stooping, I've cozily enjoyed the "feathering out" of my chicks. But suddenly, *the* day dawned—Roxane's fifteenth birthday. With that dawn, her feet hit the floor and her voice announced: "At last! Now I can get my Driver's Permit!" All too soon we joined the sizable crowd of applicants in the State Highway Department building. Daughter pencil-chewed her way through a written test while mother stood apart in a corner, hoping, alternately, for success and failure. The wide grin at test's end gave clear proof of success. (As I recall, that grin also marked the last time I saw the car keys!)

From that fateful day on, our one-on-one driver education course has been in full swing. And, although I don't have any idea how much professional driving teachers are paid, I'm convinced it's not enough! No salary could compensate for the discomfort of a 5'4" car seat adjustment on my 5'9" body: my knees are getting calluses from resting against my teeth.

No paycheck could cover the heart stoppages I've experienced there in Mergatroid's right seat. (Mergatroid being, of course, our car.) The normal, run-of-the-mill worries like falling off the roadside from overcaution or too-fast propulsion from overconfidence count for little in comparison with the weightier challenges: like our driveway. I admit, there are some natural obstacles to easy maneuvering—bushes, bank, trees, and curve. But Roxane's gleeful rise to the challenge sends me cringing to the floorboards. After the various performances of bush crushing, branch bending, bank teetering, and wild weavings, I'd probably be smarter just to close my eyes for the full length of the driveway. But that's a rather blatant admission of cowardice now, isn't it?

No profit-sharing plan could compensate for the wear and tear of avoiding all the nutty drivers who have suddenly appeared on the streets of Greenville. *How* do they so unerringly pick the precise moment to perform their wildest shenanigans for the benefit of the novice at the wheel of *our* car? Moreover, they seem to be in cahoots—I'm sure every wheel-holding madman in town comes out of his garage in response to some mysterious signal and aims for us. Even when not in motion, the enemies demonstrate their coalition against us: they park *much* too close together! After looking vainly through two complete circuits of a filled parking lot, I at last allow Roxane to aim Mergatroid at the only available space—then proceed to pray that she'll be able to find a "squeeze" gear on the indicator.

Even joint ownership of the company could provide no enticement for the parallel parking routine. So far, I've successfully ignored the necessity for such training: my ulcers aren't sufficiently calloused as yet.

They say experience is the best teacher. That's no doubt true; but it's a bit tough for us who must needs substitute for that bashful, invisible instructor. Lucky for Experience—she gets no snapped necks, gobbled nails, or nervous coronaries!

Oh yes, drive she must, if she's to keep stride with our times. And like all the other arts and techniques she's been learning over her years, this one, too, will eventually be marked "mastered" by my daughter. Meanwhile, her mother has to exhibit the difficult combination of accepting her age, recognizing her need, and responding with sound, calmly administered training. My prayers in the co-pilot's seat are not just for Roxane's immediate safety, but even more for her long-range spiritual safety. At fifteen, life itself is an unwieldy vehicle, and the challenges and dangers lurk everywhere. But, by God's grace, our daughter's "driving skills" will be directed of Him Who made and maintains the vehicle of her individuality and Who mapped the highway of service it shall take.

11
Blind

After a long and careful study, I've been forced to a difficult conclusion: my husband is blind. There is simply no other explanation for some of his most deeply-ingrained actions and attitudes. Consider, please.

Primary symptom: for the sake of an occasional headache, he resorts to aspirin. (No *that's* not the symptom of his blindness.) Unlike the feminine half of our duo, however, he has a singular inability to locate the intended remedy. The procedure is unvaryingly the same: he makes his way to the bathroom; opens the door of the medicine cabinet; slams it; rattles through the over-counter storage section; opens my bathroom closet doors; slams them; opens the medicine cabinet again; pauses; creaks the cabinet door by leaning on it; clanks the bottles and tins; slams the cabinet door; bellows: "Honey, where's the aspirin?" After 20 years of marital attachment to the man, I no longer try a vocal response, as I did early in our cohabitation. Telling him that the aspirin is in the medicine cabinet only calls forth a replay of the fruitless openings, slammings, shufflings, and clankings. Instead, I stop whatever I've been doing and go to the aid of my sight-impaired mate. Opening the medicine cabinet, I take out the aspirin bottle and place it in the husbandly hands, close the cabinet, and exit. His line for my exit? "Oh—I didn't see it." Would anyone dare suggest there is no impairment of sight?

Further symptom: when he is looking for any (repeat *any*) item of clothing, if said item is not to be found in precisely the spot it occupied yesterday, a pitiful wail erupts: "Sweetheart—where are my socks?" So again I go to the aid of the handicapped, and find the "missing" piece of apparel—after looking a fraction of an inch east or west, north or south.

Final diagnostic test: not long ago, my housecleaning efforts had filled an overlarge, unwieldy plastic bag with trash. Rather than immediately break my back carting it outside, I deposited it very nearly in the center of the kitchen floor. During the course of supper, I asked (sweetly, despite his successful circumambulation of the foreign bundle) if he would be so good as to dump the trash for me. "Sure," he replied. And that's how we left it—

and the kitchen. The following morning when I went into the kitchen to prepare breakfast, I nearly broke my neck stumbling over the trash bag. So, in the midst of readying our morning meal, I dragged the thing out to the trash can. Unable to resist a gentle wifely barb, however, I asked (*sotto voce,* of course) why he hadn't emptied the trash the night before, as promised. His reply sealed my tentative diagnosis and marked it "Final": "Oh . . . well, I came out and looked for it, but I couldn't find it."

Not only is the patient a victim of this strange disability; his handicap gives every evidence of being hereditary in the male line. Almost any time of the day or evening, one or both of our two fledgling masculine voices can be heard calling from the farthest end of the house, "Moooooooooom, where's my shirt (sneakers, basketball, notebook, deodorant . . .)?"

The chronic eye problem I've described as a physical characteristic of my husband does not, thankfully, repeat itself in his spiritual makeup. What a priceless fact that is! The Bible clearly instructs the Christian wife to be submissive and reverential to her husband. Therefore, as leader, the husband needs to have keen spiritual sight and the Christian character to act and react accordingly. I thank the Lord every day that I don't have to *hope* or *wish* for Bob's

20/20 spiritual acuity. My feminine heart can rest quietly in the knowledge of his possessing such vision—because of his daily, faithful walk in the light of God's Word.

Aspirin and socks will probably never become visible to the man of our house, but I pray that his keen sight for spiritual verity will continue undiminished.

12
Term Merchants

     Shopping trips are never more than burdensome necessities, as far as I'm concerned. I dread them. Having never been easy to fit in ready-made clothing because of my 5'9" height, any shopping stint automatically means hours wasted and temper frayed from walking, looking, and unsuccessfully trying on various outfits. My latest trip to a store brought not only tiredness, but disgust, as well.

     The try-on struggle was going about as usual and so was my patience. Then in the midst of one put-on-take-off-sigh-hang-up cycle, my eye fell upon a stenciled sign on the dressing room wall: *Security tags must be removed from garments by a sales associate.* I stopped with a dress draped over one ear: did that sign mean what I thought it meant? It did. My reaction was a mixture of disgust and sour humor. Sales associate! What it meant was a *clerk,* for pity's sake! But, like so many other institutions, individuals, and endeavors, this particular mercantile establishment had fallen prey to "verbal vagaries."

It seems that the more shallowly Americans live, the more they desire grandeur. Since substantive glory eludes their reach, a false elevation must be substituted. Pompous pretension is nowhere more evident than in the re-naming craze sweeping the land. Term merchants thrive on swapping long words for short ones, multiple wordings for single, obscure terms for clear. There is deviousness in their efforts: an attempt to disguise, hide, or dissemble. The special object of renovative wording seems to be anything that denotes a station which might appear lowly: as seen so clearly in "clerk" becoming "sales associate!" What in the world is wrong with being a clerk? Nothing. One of the busiest word markets is that having to do with women's roles: "domestic engineering" being substituted for "home economics," for instance. Malarkey! I'm *not* a domestic engineer (or anything even approaching any kind of an engineer!)—I'm an ordinary *housewife,* and that title brings both pleasure and pride.

Any hint of servitude seems to be particularly horrific to the sensibility of term merchants.

Evidently, ours should be a classless society. For that very reason, we who know the Lord need to hold on to the older, soundly sensible terms which give accurate identification. Why should we join the ranks of those who exult in obscuring meaning, disguising motives, and reaching for nonexistent "equality"?

Even more important, we believers should avoid language usage which makes servanthood distasteful. Aren't we, after all, *supposed* to be servants? Indeed: servants first of all to our Saviour, and then servants of fellow believers. But I wonder if some of us haven't been trapped in the "terms maze" and staggered out on the other side of it with an inflated opinion of ourselves and our worth to the Lord's service: maybe, for instance, we've let "deacon's wife" or "Christian teacher" or "minister's wife" take on a modernized connotation which places us somehow in a superior position. Yet the basic intention for every such ministry is *service*.

If in some unguarded moment I should become enamored of a high-sounding title, I pray that the Lord will bring to mind that ridiculous dressing room sign, "sales associate," and remind me thereby of the deceptiveness of terms. May any self-exaltation be immediately punctured, and may I, instead, exult in the blessed expectation of that moment at Eternity's dawn when I hope to hear my blessed

Saviour say, "Well done, thou good and faithful *servant.*"

13
Surprise Ending

Chalk up another one for the "BPJ BLOOPERS" chart. Like so many others before it, this flub had the uneasy characteristic of publicity. Fortunately, however, its applied lesson came privately.

There we all were, gathered around the supper table. The table itself had been extended to its greatest length in order to accommodate 1) our daughter's girlfriend, who was spending the week with us, and 2) three new students who were to be our "campus children" for the year. The meal had already had some shaky moments—caused, notably, by the madly smoking but barely cooking charcoal grill. As a result, the hamburgers were not only tardy; they were decidedly underdone. Having adjusted nobly to that introductory sally, our young guests relaxed, and all of us enjoyed eating and visiting. I approached the dessert preparations with a modicum of confidence (*that* rare commodity should have been a warning in itself!); the freshly baked cake looked and smelled just right; dishing up the accompanying ice cream promised to be pleasantly simple.

It wasn't until all nine spoons dipped into the ice cream and carried it to nine expectant mouths that the disappointing truth struck home: the ice cream was *old*. Mental argument that the carton had come from the store only 3½ hours earlier couldn't change the tasted fact: the ice cream had aged to the point of strange taste and repulsive texture. There was no room for remedy, but room aplenty for apology.

It was during the post-party clean-up that the puzzle was solved: the ice cream boo-boo had been mine, not the store's. Opening the freezer compartment of the refrigerator, I found myself staring straight at an unopened carton of buttered almond ice cream. Disbelieving the testimony of sight, I then opened the full-size upright freezer. Sure enough, there was the ice cream carton from which I'd taken our dessert. The two containers were the same, but the contents were vastly different. Having forgotten there even was an old carton, I'd mistakenly reached for the wrong ice cream in the wrong freezer. The result: an unpleasantly memorable dessert.

The old ice cream immediately bit the dust (or, more accurately, was bitten by the garbage disposal). As that cooperative mechanism digested the offending dessert, my heart was ingesting a spiritual lesson.

Those ice cream cartons were identical in every way externally—same size, same shape, same label, same flavor, same store markings. Internally, however, they were quite unalike. Doesn't that accurately describe what we experience in the life of our souls? Outwardly, we appear to be the same from day to day. Family and friends take it for granted that they know what we have inside. But how easy it is for us to hide behind packaging! Though we walk, talk, and look the way we always have, our spiritual contents may very well be shrunken, flavorless, and gritty. Ideally, our contents are of such quality and flavor that others are nourished and refreshed thereby. But too often a seeking heart is left hungry, and a wounded spirit unrefreshed, because we've allowed our spiritual contents to dry up. Like ice cream, spirituality is not a once-and-for-all concern. Instead, freshness is a matter of renewal. May our packaging be a true indicator of contents kept fresh daily by the renewal possible only through close fellowship with the Lord Jesus Christ.

14
What's in a Name

It made me, somehow, different—
therefore I resented and disliked it. Earnest
questioning of my parents brought understanding to the intellect, but not to the heart.
Nor could the unspoken queries find their
desired resolution; no, this thing was insep-
arably a part of me.

It gave other people fits, as well: teachers
frowned, hesitated, or sighed when they discov-
ered it; my peers valiantly ignored it. Under the
impact of such overwhelming confirmation of
oddity, I decided to pursue the only escape
route possible: atrophy through disuse.

The "it" referred to in the paragraphs above
is my given name, Beneth. All my childhood
longing in the world could not make it a nice,
sensible, *simple* "Mary" or "Ann." Pronounced
correctly with two short e's and the first syllable
accented, it was less offensive than the man-

glings it consistently endured. There were whole years in grade school when I was BenETHed by the teacher. Then there were the less frequent but more memorably unpleasant occasions when my name and I were "put down" by the BeNEATH pronunciation. Not only were accent and vowel sounds altered: some inventive souls daringly took the plunge into pronunciation by rearranging the syllables (more to their personal liking, presumably) as, for example, in BEN-THA.

My parents, perhaps trying to compensate for their original, imaginative but burdensome choice, obligingly substituted "Benny" at home. Recognizing the alias as the best chance likely to be offered, I took it to my bosom (or at least to my writing hand). Then as femininity slowly replaced tomboyishness, the -y ending struck me as being unladylike. So for several years Bennie became the favored orthography. In the teen years, however, that suffix seemed uncolorful, and I experimented with Benni and Benne, finally settling on the latter.

Now for the confession: having survived into middle age, I've had my emotional equilibrium jarred by a belated *fondness* for my original, whole, unaltered name of Beneth. Ironically, the mutilated version has taken such firm hold in the minds of family and friends that few if any will make the effort to adjust. Therefore, by not valuing my name properly, I've made myself immeasurably poorer. Regrettably, the devalued coin of a nickname threatens to jingle irritatingly in my mental pockets forever after.

Just as a temporal name can be mistreated and distorted by its bearer, so too can our eternal name. What do we do with the name of Christ we bear? Some light valuation may come, at first, simply from spiritual immaturity. Just as a child may at first mispronounce his own name, so a young Christian can be expected to make some blunders in living for the Lord. But as with the physical child, so with the spiritual—one of his earliest concerns will be for the proper enunciation of the name by which he's known. If that concern is not soon evident in a Christian, his growth is not what it ought to be. And as the years progress, the consistency and clarity of our pronunciation should steadily increase. We "pronounce" our Christianity by the vowels of attitude, the consonants of action, and the accents of associations.

Though there is sadness in recognizing the abuse to and waste of my given name, a far greater cause for sorrow would be the misuse of that blessed name *Christian*—the name borne by the grace and for the testimony of the Lord Jesus Christ. I yearn to pronounce it, protect it, and propagate it with faithful, joyful correctness.

15
Daffodils

One of the loveliest pictures hanging in the gilt frame of my childhood memories is that of the Daffodil House. The work, a bright landscape, has long been a part of my mental gallery; only recently, however, has the caption been supplied.

As a child whose sisters were in school and whose brother was still in his crib, much of my play consisted of wandering through the woods of Washington state's coastal region near our home. Those woods provided contentment in being alone in the fragrant, sun-dappled world of the evergreen forests, and excitement over the never-ending discoveries opening there to my eyes.

One spring day, the near woods offered little that was new, so I extended my ramblings. After a considerable time of log-balancing, moss-inspecting, bark-feeling, and flower-discovering, I came abruptly upon a clearing. At first, its newness startled me into realizing I'd wandered far from familiar territory. But shining through the trees was a scene which irresistibly drew me from the sheltering evergreens. In the middle of the clearing stood a house: but what a house it was! Small, gray, delapidated, it had obviously stood vacant for many years. Those untended years were written in the weather-silvered boards, the staring windows, and the tilted frame. At the same time, however, there was also evidence that someone, sometime, had tended that house; had occupied the hollow rooms and had lent life and laughter to the premises. That evidence spread over the entire clearing: a carpet of glowing, golden daffodils. Shag carpet it was, with the buttery expanse stretching from one wall of evergreens to the other.

The exultant reveling in beauty that scene afforded seemed peculiarly mine for a number of years. Then, in high school, a literary work so accurately captured that well-remembered scene and reaction that it caught my breath away: it was William Wordsworth's poem, "The Daffodils." Despite the accuracy of the lines, however, the title for my personal picture of daffodils is not taken from Wordsworth's poem. Instead, the caption has been written by the

Lord, and it makes of memory's painting a blue-print for spiritual inspiration: *Bequest.*

For each of us who know the Lord Jesus Christ as Saviour, life can be rightly termed God's gift: a plot of time's ground, so to speak. Ours is the choice what and how we shall build thereon. Many of us build only with an eye to the present, erecting a dwelling that is adequate—or perhaps even luxurious—for immediate physical needs. Now and then, however, there is a Christian whose greater wisdom sees past the walls of self and out into the expanse on either side—arable acres upon which he may make spiritual plantings. Not only will he, his family, and friends enjoy the resultant color and aroma; after he vacates time's plot, unknown future wanderers will have unrefutable proof that bulbs planted with the hoe of faith bear colorful blossoms of continuing testimony.

Every passing year more clearly demonstrates to me the transience of earthly life and clarifies the need for so living with that forward-looking wisdom, that those who come after, not recognizing a name or revering an accomplishment, may, instead, rejoice in the bequest of spiritual beautification.

16
Relative Positions

Somewhere, sometime recently, while going about a day's normal routine, I glanced down at my hands in a quiet moment and saw something unnoticed until then, but much-contemplated since. A simple, taken-for-granted thing, its significance is especially pertinent to the day in which we live: the relative position of an engagement and wedding ring. Look at your own left hand third finger for a moment, then think with me through some of the encouragements and challenges to be drawn from the rings—inanimate but eloquent—upon it.

I distinctly remember when, back in my teens, I challenged the newly heard explanation for the engagement ring being worn outermost; wasn't that positioning backwards? After all, the diamond in the engagement ring is worth a lot more than the simple gold of the wedding band! Today, however, twenty-plus years of marriage have shown how appropriate that traditional position is: the color and sparkle of the romantic symbol stands sentinel to the plain solidity of the vows' binding.

Certainly in a time when so much of Satan's heavy artillery is bombarding the institution of marriage generally and Christian marriage particularly, we Christian wives would do well to reinforce our acknowledgement of and attention to our marriage relationship itself. No matter how busy our lives, no matter how varied and constant the demands upon us, we nevertheless need to realize that our *marriage itself* is the most important consideration facing us. Yet it's so easy to get our eyes on the shiny things of life and off the solid things. And *that's* when the devil will manage to dent or even dissolve the fundamental entity we've been taking for granted.

Remember the newness, the excitement and fun of newlywed days? Remember what a delight it was to pour concentration and energy into simply "wife-ing it"? But sit quietly and ask yourself a hard question, as I've been doing: now that we're several (or many) years into marriage, has wifehood deteriorated into something that comes second, third, or even farther down the line of priorities?

No one in her right mind would deny that other concerns have to enter into the picture: home, friendships, children, church, etc. And to ignore any of those would be wrong. *But*—each of those, though valuable, should take only "guard duty" position for our marriage relationship itself. It's clear in God's Word that the "leaving and cleaving" descriptive of marriage in the Garden of Eden is to continue to be a woman's primary area of responsibility. Humanly speaking, her *husband* is her number one project.

To bring the matter down onto a more everyday level, I've constructed a little quiz posing some "story problems" to check up on myself. Perhaps you'll find it adaptable to your situation, too:

1. I'm in the middle of housework; just in the middle of a spurt of efficiency and accomplishment. My husband walks in or telephones and says, "Honey, let's take the car and go ..." How do I answer? Frankly, the first inclination may be to say, "Oh, not *now,* dear ..." all the while justifying my common sense choice. Common sense? Well, maybe, but this is where *uncommon* sense should come into play—so I drop the broom, dust cloth, or whatever, and go spend that time with my husband.

2. The kitchen is topsy-turvy with obvious feverish activity on one or more Scout projects.

With glue under my fingernails, exhaustion's glaze on my eyeballs, and my elbow holding a drying project section together, I hear a childish voice call, "Hey, Mom, Dad would like to come home for an early supper!" Do I do the obvious thing and tell him to fix himself a sandwich, or am I sensitive to the *easily obscured* need to clear the decks for a supper invasion?

3. I've been on a special, day-long shopping trip with "the girls." By evening, the major acquisition is tired feet and tense nerves. Through the fog of exhaustion comes the query, "Honey, how about pressing that blue suit for me to wear tomorrow?" The natural reaction might be, "*How* can he expect that after a day like I've had? After all, there are other suits in his closet...." But, instead, shouldn't I reach for *supernatural* reaction, forget about my hurting feet, and think instead of his heart's hurt should I refuse?

4. The church's Women's Missionary Circle is demanding more and more time, since I've had several years in a row of being an officer. So, when Hubby suggests a spur-of-the-moment guest meal for Tuesday evening, the ordinary comeback might be, "Not *that* evening! After all, as president of the WMC ..." How much wiser the *extra*ordinary preference for being queen at home!

In each of the above imagined-but-pertinent

situations, I could lean hard on excuses such as, "His timing is so *dumb*. Those Scout merit badges are really important to the boys. But it's always when I'm the most tired or busy ... Well, really (with loud sigh inserted), I suppose I should concentrate more on being accommodating." But wait—can excuses or good intentions ever compensate for *misplaced values?*

God Himself recognized the importance of proper wifely wisdom. That fact is clear in the second chapter of Titus, where He inspired the Apostle Paul to urge older Christian women to teach the younger women "to be sober (that is, self-disciplined), to love their husbands, to love their children"—right there, our priorities are established.

So constant is the challenging of our priorities, so vital our proper maintenance of them, that we need more than occasional reminders—we need *daily tutoring*. Such private instructions may very well be at hand—in the form of our nearer-to-the-heart, diamond-guarded wedding band.

17
Words of Wisdom

It was just a little wooden sign hanging in an ice cream store, but it struck—and stuck with—me because of its succinctness and accuracy. The title read, *Four things a woman ought to know:* Then came a list of feminine requirements: 1. How to dress like a girl. 2. How to act like a lady. 3 How to think like a man. 4. How to work like a horse. Cute and catchy, isn't it? Indeed—but it's also, though blunt, surprisingly correct. After copying the list and tucking it away in my wallet, I've had several occasions on which I've mentally clothed those skeletal thoughts with application's flesh.

1. How to dress like a girl. Was there ever an age when that urging toward femininity in appearance was more appropriate? On every side we see the sad effects of unisex and sloppi-

ness—both of which are mortal enemies of pleasing, appropriate feminine appearance. But that very decline makes it even more important that a born-again woman hold to womanliness in dress. Who but an enemy of the Creator God would delight in trying to rub out the lines of demarcation and role-identity He has established? Honoring and preserving the distinctives imposed by our Maker is an inherent part of our testimony. Without going overboard into Scripture-distorting emphases, modesty and femininity should always mesh in the appearance of a blood-cleansed woman.

2. How to act like a lady. Ah, yes. Here's another "out-of-date" consideration in a do-your-own-thing world. Words like "manners" and "decorum" are foreign to the world's tongue. Unspoken by the world, perhaps—but we who know the Lord Jesus Christ certainly have a responsibility to enunciate them clearly—because ladylike conduct has its roots in consideration for others: the "discretion" principle so clearly established in God's Word.

3. How to think like a man. Although for this particular point there is no clear-cut scriptural principle extant, it most certainly is a practical suggestion! Our daily associations with the masculine gender (beginning with and including those of about the age of two) should convince us how unlike masculine mental processes are

to feminine. There are, of course, many facets to this jewel of differentiation—but it can be generally categorized as male *logic* vs. female *emotionalism*. As the physical, so too the mental differences have been built into us by God—and we would avoid many misunderstandings, clashes, and hurt feelings by always taking the masculine viewpoint into account. That will help us understand, for example:

—how he can totally forget the spat at breakfast (whereas you simmer unhappily over it all day)

—why he reacts calmly under "small" pressures, and just "rolls with the punches" (while you're coming unglued and noting that punches are always a lot easier on the referee than on the contender)

—why he looks at you with blank amazement when you burst into tears over scorched potatoes

4. How to work like a horse. Inelegant, but accurate. Although there are unnumbered comic allusions to the "little woman" and her sundry roles as cook, maid, nurse, gardener, bookkeeper, baby-sitter, *et al.*, it's nevertheless true: although we don't spend eight hours a day digging ditches, a woman's life consists largely of *work*. Every assignment is mentally, physically, and/or emotionally demanding, and the salary is never countable in dollars and cents!

Well, then, can we justifiedly kick, scream, or complain over the lack of take-home pay? Certainly not—the *home itself* is our pay! No richer remuneration exists under the sun.

How soon, or at what age, a girl should become acquainted with this list would be, of course, open for debate. However, from the looks of things in today's Christian world, I'd say, "The sooner the better!" All too often we mothers of daughters tend toward contentment with inevitability rather than contending for indoctrination. In other words, we operate on the assumption, "She'll learn all the realities of womanhood when she gets there," rather than "It's my responsibility to prepare her ahead of time." The latter, obviously, calls for a great deal more effort on our part both in precept and in practice. But the longer I live, the more firmly I'm convinced that such active inoculation against misapprehension is not only the wiser choice, but also the necessary one. That conviction comes as a result of talking to many disenchanted young women who wail, "But I never dreamed ..." or "This is not what I'd expected at all." Youth's tendency is to idealize, to romanticize—leaving itself open to varying degrees of letdown when reality presents itself. Mature parental obligation, therefore, would decree that we instruct without injuring, and prepare without paralyzing.

Toward that end, with our own fledgling
female, I've asked the Lord to help me tack this
little four-point list on the walls of my
consciousness. May it, along with that well-
marked, well-loved 31st chapter of Proverbs,
become an ever-present spiritual challenge—
underlined, however, with a chuckle.

18
Spilled Milk

Have you ever lived in a travel trailer, camper, or motor home for any length of time? Our family has. During two summers, we traveled for six-week periods in a motor home. Though the many miles of gray highway have been left behind, the touring tutelage has taken up permanent residence here in the stationary-but-not-static moments of today.

Motor home travel held special challenges for us, both as a family unit and as individuals. The basic consideration was simple occupancy: five human beings, none of whom could be described as diminutive, experiencing the 24-hour-a-day habitation of an outwardly monstrous, inwardly midget box on wheels. Besides and appurtenant to our living bodies was an impressive collection of paraphernalia: shoes, books, socks, toys, sweaters, cooking utensils, clothing, food, cosmetics, maps, and small appliances, to name only a few. The second challenge was the amount of space into which all the above necessarily had to fit (tightly!): 25 feet—shared with such life-sustaining equipment as engine, steering/riding accommodations, sink, stove, refrigerator, storage, bathroom, closet, eating area, and beds. Therefore, the physical distribution on the aforementioned equipment resulted in a "free space" only inches wide—the aisle running the length of the vehicle. All of this compactness demanded tremendous coordination of activities and even movement. There were times when we wished for the ability to choreograph our breathing! In a word, our summer trips had us *really* together.

Looming out of the general landscapes of yesterday's travel are some mountainous specific incidents which continue to act as landmarks for today's basically immobile existence. One such experience occurred at some now-forgotten spot in the West.

It had been a long day's drive; all of us were tired and hungry; therefore, impatience was prowling on a flimsy chain. Once we'd reached our evening's destination and the men had managed the motor home's various umbilical attachments, Roxane and I began preparing the evening meal. While the fact boded promise for our mid-sections, it did absolutely nothing for our nerves, thanks to the almost nonexistent cooking "space," the hunger-hovering boys, and the setting of the ever-wobbly table. Finally, though, we began the meal itself. Its start was signalled by the usual repetitious warnings to "Be careful!" The slick table surface, the unsteady central support, and the crowded eating area made all the warnings eminently sensible. The meal was scarcely under way when our youngest managed to circumvent all precautions—he performed a dramatically thorough spilling of his drink. While three of us hustled to capture the runaway milk, the head of the house launched into exhaustion-sparked remonstrance dotted with the parental queries both of us were entertaining: "Didn't we tell you to be careful?" "Why do you do so much spilling?" With trembling lip and crestfallen expression, Stephen offered the only reply he could dredge up from a mortified heart: " 'Cause I'm a kid, I guess."

Although that particular phrase has not passed Stephen's lips again since that summer evening, it has often traversed my heart. Ah, indeed, kids *are* kids—and despite pressures of shrinking time versus bloating responsibility, we who are parents would do well to remember that fact. Yet, simple though it may be, that one indisputable verity all too often looses from its moorings and floats off beyond the horizon of our mental focus. Recognizing the inescapable childishness of childhood helps retain the flexibility and imagination to make allowances for those short folks who inhabit its world. I've found that when I most firmly hang on to the concept of my children's immaturity I'm most able to relax into enjoying these special, ever-changing creatures who share our home. That enjoyment extends to the necessary *under-taking* which must be done in behalf of their puerility.

The lessons which spilled into my conscious-ness with our little boy's milk has not only acted as an antacid for my in-house attitude; it has also formed a pool reflecting a wider scene: the household of faith. It is all too easy for us who have known the Lord a considerable length of time to manifest either impatience or super-ciliousness toward our younger brothers and sisters in Christ. Our attitude fairly bristles with complaint about their need to grow up. It is much wiser, harder, and more needful, how-ever, to *contribute* to that desired growth.

As we did that evening in the motor home, so we need to do among our Christian compan-ions—patiently "wipe up the spills," and lovingly bind up the spirits.

19
Point of View

Point of view. That's a common term, one that most of us use rather frequently in daily conversation. But just the other week the impact of its meaning hit me full force.

Summer this year meant that our two older children acquired full-time jobs. Since our youngest was only ten, he was, of course, unable to sign on with any of the various campus work crews. The fact that he felt left out soon became apparent in his long face, his restlessness in the sibling-bare house, and his wildly impractical schemes for money-making. Out of sympathy (and desperation), I concocted a plan: Stephen would become my household helper—doing things like dusting and vacuuming, wastebasket emptying, and handkerchief ironing—for a weekly fee.

The venture began auspiciously enough.

Stephen appeared suitably impressed with my informal lecture on the need for consistency, thoroughness, and initiative. The first week's accomplishment was pleasing to both of us, too. But then came Monday of the second week. One of the chores assigned for that day was vacuuming the living room and dining room. Resting in the former week's performance, I trusted my half-pint assistant to do an acceptable job. Some time after the vacuum's humming and the boy's whistling had stopped, and "Finished, Mom!" had been proclaimed, I took a trip through the living room. Disappointment met me at the door: the job had been only partially done. Although the vacuum's path was agreeably thorough in the middle of the room, the outer edges were untouched. Calling Stephen from his play, I took him into the living room. Words of disapproval for a poorly executed task were met by proclamations of innocence and insult. To put an end to the matter, I instructed Stephen to stand on a straight chair. He did so. "Now, Son, look again at the job you've done." His sheepish expression acknowledged the incriminating evidence, and he moved silently to redo the vacuuming. *His efforts had been revealed and redirected by a changed point of view.*

A little boy, a vacuum cleaner, and a carpet: the Lord used them as a microcosmic lecture.

For many of us, the "first week" of our Christian experience was marked by industry, thoroughness, and high spirits. As we learned our spiritual "job assignments," we responded with eager dedication. But would an honest comparison between those days and our present Christian lives reveal a decrease in our faithfulness?

The rooms of spiritual responsibility for each of us are many—and the longer we've lived in them, the easier it is to rely upon habit; to excuse our hurried or halfhearted efforts; to inspect our doings from a low-level viewpoint.

Just as I hoisted Stephen onto that dining room chair last summer, so do I need the Lord to lift me to a spiritual elevation from which I can see as *He* sees—and thereby realize that I've been stopping short of edges, turned aside by objects, hence leaving my heaven-directed tasks poorly or partially done.

The elevated viewpoint cannot be gained by Self's clambering onto a rickety stool of positive thinking or the wobbly stilts of "deeper life" emphasis—rather, it can rightly come only as I allow God Himself, working through His Word, to lift me onto the firm height of *thinking His thoughts after Him.*

In this hallway called Today, may the Lord give each of us Christian women the grace to look back upon rooms marred by short strokes of effort as incentive toward genuine repentance; then, gazing into the rooms of opportunity ahead, dedicate ourselves to testimonial endeavor which will be unstinting in its efforts, thorough in its coverage, and all-encompassing in its effectiveness.

20
Traces of Salt

Aren't you thankful the Lord doesn't limit His teachings to monumental public presentations? Instead, the principles of His Word are reinforced and made personal through the minutes and hours of every day as we walk with Him—written with the ink of the ordinary and set forth in the script of the seemingly insignificant. Such an experience came my way just the other day.

I was going through the usual early-morning routine at my dressing table. After completing face care and hairdo preparation, I began that final preparatory activity—vision adjustment. Equipment for managing contact lenses is quite unexceptional: a hand mirror, lint-free towel, and container of saline solution. Being a novice in the ranks of contact lens users, I meticulously follow the prescribed routine of lens care and application. It had never occurred to me to question the truth of the label on that opaque plastic bottle claiming to contain "saline solution." Curiosity felt a vague tickling, though, when repeated handling of the stuff made it appear to be no different from ordinary water.

On this particular morning I squeezed a teaching for my heart out of that plastic bottle. Whether carelessness or haste caused me to drop some of the saline solution on my hand mirror, a demands-packed morning prevented my washing the drops away. Besides, water always dries, right? Oh yes, the drops did dry— but by so doing they verified the character of that clear solution: where each drop had been that morning, there was a *trace of salt* in the afternoon. What a lesson plan unfolded there!

Traces of salt. Aren't we Christians called "the salt of the earth"? Assuredly. Moreover, study, experience, and sermons have pointed out to each of us that salt has certain characteristics and uses: among other things, it adds flavor and zest to foods and acts as a preservative or spoilage retardant.

Traces of salt. I wonder if you and I, ordinary Christian women, leave such identifying traces in the places we visit and upon the lives we touch each day. It's easy to convince ourselves that the only "important" testimonies are those borne by preachers, evangelists, and full-time Christian workers. But that feeling evaporates in the burning truth of God's Word: *every one of us* has an obligation to leave traces of salt wherever he goes. Our doing so is an imperative—because each has a unique circle of activity and acquaintance—a circle in which the only or the outstanding saltiness is yours or mine. What's in that circle? The grocery and department stores where we shop; the medical and business offices we frequent; the city block or country lane where we live; the homes we visit. Are the forever-living souls within that circle even aware of the fact that we are spiritual salt? Or does our conduct and conversation attest to an essence as insubstantial and colorless as their own?

Traces of salt. Not truckloads. We're not to shout a five-point outline in each building we enter or to each person we meet. In fact, salt in oversize quantities is self-defeating. That fact was "salted away" in my consciousness a couple of years ago: our household got a spur-of-the-moment yen for homemade ice cream, so I asked one of our older children to run to the store for some ice cream salt. He came home with a 25 pound bag of it! Needless to point out, that bag lies virtually untouched to this day.

Traces of salt. God simply wants our lives as born-again women to be so consistent with the standards of Scripture, so lovely with the radiance of the Saviour, that they leave traces of salt—salt which the Holy Spirit can use to create thirst for the Water of Life.

21
Slip-ups

There's a very ordinary, oft-occurring incident that has been brought freshly (and blushingly) to my attention. Any woman reading this column should be able to empathize with both the occurrence itself and the resultant sensations. Okay, so what is it? That public moment when someone approaches you to murmur, "Did you know that your slip is showing?" Or to reach up and tuck under the facing and tag at the back of your neckline. Or to report that you have a run in your stockings. Now I ask you, is there anyone who can't identify with such a happening? Let's walk together through a verbal replay in order to identify the incident's parts and its impartings.

When your informant approaches, you turn to her in expectation of pleasantries about to be exchanged. Her word or action, however, results in your exhuming your social unease. The typical immediate reaction is mortification. *"How long* have I been walking around like that? Congratulations, Queen of the Sloppies!" or "Yipes, am I ever embarrassed! Great way to make a good impression; oh for a good, deep hole to crawl into!" or "Why did she even have to tell me?"

Eventually, after the flush of mortification has faded somewhat, we have a secondary reaction: gratification. Belatedly, perhaps, but surely, we recognize the fact that the experience has been beneficial. First, it has given us an "others" viewpoint, reminding us that we don't see ourselves as others see us. Second, it has motivated us toward being more careful in checking details we otherwise might skip. And, finally, this embarrassing-but-enlightening happening has enabled us to correct the thing that was wrong.

Such a "slip-ery" experience is not only educational in its primary sphere as just discussed; it also has application as to the habiliment of the soul. Pride and self-satisfaction would make me think I'm pretty well "decked out" in a garment that is well-fitting, clean, and mended. Then a phrase from the Word of God or a whisper from the Holy Spirit nudges me into realizing that all is *not* well. And sure enough, the spiritual reactions follow the same patterning as did the social.

In the mortification phase there is the discomfort of having to acknowledge something askew. Then comes the hot flush of realizing that others must have been aware of and perhaps were offended by the fault. Ah, and shame? It makes me want to hide in a corner. Then comes the rueful wondering why that particular Scripture passage had to leap unexpectedly to my attention just when it did.

At last, as the uncomfortable squirmings subside, gratification makes its calming entrance. How sobering it is to see my soul's dress, not from the customary, limited viewpoint, but from the elevated, concentrated perspective from which God Himself inspects it! Could there be any stronger reminder to tighten up on daily self-inspection? And finally, my heart's reactions come to that point for which the Lord has patiently waited: the end of reaction and the beginning of action—positive action which will result in my (a) adjusting the length of my "slips," (b) neatening my "facings," and (c) mending my "snags" and "runs."

Only as my ever-seeing Heavenly Father points out "slip-ups" in my spiritual dress can that lovely garment of salvation be protected from the scruffiness that Satan so untiringly works to produce.

22
Time Tested

     Due to the ever-changing, unpre-
dictable, and often-conflicting schedules kept by
the occupants of our house, we depend heavily
upon calendars and clocks. So heavily, in fact,
that we keep several calendars activated, and
hardly any room in the house is without its own
clock. After twenty-odd years of this challenging life, I've grown accustomed to living with
one eye on those various indicators of time.

    Yet, no matter how dedicated my efforts for
productive scheduling, the inescapable fact is
that *tempus fugit*. And, while it's *fugit*-ing,
it's also being *used against me* by Satan.
How craftily the devil uses time! He is *par
excellence* at time management—for my testimonial manglement.

    Calendars and clocks? Satan utilizes both in
what might be called his "pre" attacks. Surely
you've noticed how gleefully active he gets in
times of pre-blessing, pre-opportunity, pre-

spiritual responsibility. The following personal example may run parallel to your own experiences.

Pre-blessing. Just before those outstanding times of spiritual refreshment (Thanksgiving, Christmas, Bible Conference, etc.), the devil wallops me with such weariness of mind that bright prospects suddenly dim; eagerness flip-flops into endurance (with emphasis on the "end").

Pre-opportunity. A ladies retreat marked on the calendar reminds Satan that it's time to whack me with fearful palpitations: timidity's terrors over traveling alone, personal incapabilities, and meeting and ministering to strangers bludgeon anticipation into anxiety.

Pre-spiritual responsibility. On this one, the devil must be consulting a stopwatch! Every Monday evening of the academic year a friend and I team teach a two-hour class called The Minister's Wife. By midmorning on Mondays, I can count on being bopped with the brickbat of self-pity ("Monday is *such* an awful, busy, tired day anyway!"), and noon finds me fairly mummified with self-doubt ("These things we're teaching are going to have a lifelong effect on these girls! How can someone as failure filled as I dare to present such material!").

The "posts" are no less skillfully used against us by Satan.

Post-spiritual refreshment. A retreat or other special meeting comes to an end. In the course of the meetings the Lord's working has been evident and exciting, making you determine to claim and pursue spiritual victory. You need hardly even open the front door of the house before a well-timed barrage of "mountaintop-to-mundane" cannon balls decimate your determination.

Post-service. You've just finished delivering a devotional talk toward which you'd worked and prayed for weeks. What's the devil's time-tested weapon here? Criticism! Someone from the audience approaches to say, "You really had a lot of trouble getting your thoughts together on your second point, didn't you?" Wham!—time-bomb detonation.

Post-victory. You've been rejoicing in a major answer to prayer or a much-sought spiritual self-conquest. Delightedly busy at his "post," Satan not only has his eye on the grandfather clock, but he also has his thumb on the stopwatch so that he knows just the moment to whack you from one side with pricked spirits and from the other side with inflating pride!

Our Archenemy is indeed a master of time management. So what is the Christian woman to do? *First*, recognize the reality of his "time-tested" battle tactics; that denies him the element of surprise. Second, strengthen defenses by locating past-proven weaknesses in order to arm them with multiple layers of God's Word. Finally, since there's no way to avoid the timetraps altogether, determine, by God's grace, to move through them. Unscathed? Perhaps not—but certainly wiser and stronger; more knowledgeable of our Enemy's and our Defender's powers.

Calendar pages turning. Clocks ticking and chiming. Both remind us of two incontrovertible, encouraging facts: not only will the devil's battle time eventually end, but also—right now, in the hot-and-heavy battle days—"My *times* are in thy hand" (Psalm 31:15).

23
Preserves

Recently, when we entertained a friend's family for a meal, the wife presented us with a two-quart jar of raspberries she had canned during the summer. As I placed that mouthwatering hostess gift in the kitchen cupboard among other jars of varying sizes and contents, a phrase from my devotional reading in the little book of Jude flashed into my mind: " ... sanctified by God the Father, and preserved in Jesus Christ ..."

As homemakers, you and I can relate to the word "preserved" in a very down-to-earth way. Not only did our mothers and grandmothers preserve foods by canning, but many of us are resurrecting the art as we try to hold down living expenses.

Preserved. What a marvelous word as it applies to our Christian lives! God promises that we who know Him by salvation through His Son, the Lord Jesus Christ, will be *preserved!* First of all, *we are preserved from hell.* Romans 8:1 tells us, "There is therefore now no condemnation to them which are in Christ Jesus, who walk not after the flesh, but after the Spirit." Second, *we're promised preservation from overwhelming temptation:* I Corinthians 10:13 says, "There hath no temptation taken you but such as is common to man: but God is faithful, who will not suffer you to be tempted above that ye are able; but will with the temptation also make a way to escape, that ye may be able to bear it." And third, *we are preserved for the completion of His will in our lives and service:* I Thessalonians 5:23 and 24: "And the very God of peace sanctify you wholly; and I pray God your whole spirit and soul and body be preserved blameless unto the coming of our Lord Jesus Christ. Faithful is he that calleth you, who also will do it."

What blessed preservation you and I have by God's own hand! But, I wonder, "What kind of preserves are we?" Just as on a pantry shelf we can see any variety of preserved foods, so too is there tremendous variation among Christian ("preserved") women. Let's ask the Lord to make us do some serious contemplation from a seemingly simple comparison.

Maybe we're pickles. When you get right down to it, there is an over-abundance of *that* type of preserve in Christian circles! But how can we recognize ourselves as spiritual pickles? Let's check up against the following characteristics:

Saturated with the brine of negativism.

Flavored with the dillweed of complaint.

Reeking with the garlic of self-righteousness.

The "pickle" Christian woman has made the water of God's Word into something it was never intended to be—an acidic entity which puckers, warps, and shrinks her while repelling those around her.

Ideally, of course, our marvelous preservation by the Lord ought to result in our being *spiritual peaches*. Yet how pitifully few of this type of "preserve" we find in our fundamental churches! The characteristics of these rare, exemplary Christian women are markedly unlike their pickled sisters. Their minds and spirits are suspended in and sweetened by the delicate syrup of God's grace. Having allowed that grace to permeate their entire beings, "peach" Christians exude the genuine sweetness of the Spirit rather than the saccharine of self. Their aspect is consistently and pleasantly attractive: preservation has softened, not shrunk, them. The nourishment they offer is delicately blended and balanced—measured out accurately from the cup of living obedience to God's Word. Moreover the *joy* of obedience enhances their flavor, and they exude the spicy tang of individuality and laughter.

Our preservation at the hand of the Lord Jesus Christ certainly should be a constant source of exultation for each of us. Just as certainly, it should be the motivator for examination as to our use or abuse of preservation. Let's ask the Lord to subject us to the boiling pressure of conviction, then to label and date the product of His dealings, that we may ever after be reminded how essential it is to be *peach preserves.*

24
The Manx

Do you know what a Manx is? It's a type of domestic cat—a cat characterized, outstandingly, by taillessness. A couple of years ago, a Manx came into our lives; when she left, she had accomplished a mission to my interior.

That little cat's appearance was completely unbidden. Suddenly she just was there—"there" being the front door of our family room. Sitting on our stoop, she looked up into our surprised faces with the calm self-possession which said, "Well, it's about time you opened that door." There was no identification on her, and inspection found her to be pretty much what she'd appeared to be at first—a small, jet black, female cat; a diminutive feline with wobbly hind quarters.

That little black cat's chances for adoption

by the Joneses were inauspicious in the extreme. In the first place, our big white cat, Charlemagne, didn't like the interloper one little bit, and he tried repeatedly to drive her away. Second, we didn't need another cat. Third, my husband staunchly held to the tenet that we didn't need *any* cat; that in spite of the fact we'd nurtured Charlemagne to a healthy and proud prime, he (Bob, that is) continued as an unconverted cat-hater. It was upon the axis of that latter contention that the little world of Manx-vs.-man began to turn.

First rotation. Bob's head-of-the-house injunctives began vehemently: "Don't anyone *dare* feed that stray!" A few days later, "We simply can't feed that creature—why, it'll never leave if we do." Later still, "Well, maybe just a *little* food; it must be pretty hungry—but *don't* ever let it inside!"

Second rotation. "Boy, it's really cold this morning. Er—isn't there a basket or box somewhere around the house? We could at least keep the rain off this silly cat."

Third rotation. "Oh, I don't suppose it will hurt to let her in for a *little* while in the early evenings—only if Charlemagne's out wandering somewhere, of course, and only in *this* room."

Full and continuing rotation. Once inside, Coal Dust (the cat we absolutely were *not* going to keep) took on Bob as a special project. Her knock-off-that-big-fellow campaign each evening made for quite a performance! She'd wait until the moment when he had the newspaper open and his mind concentrated upon its contents; she'd uncurl from whatever lap she'd been occupying, stretch with elaborate nonchalance, then make a straightforward approach to her quarry. She'd settle—only touching his foot ever so slightly—to clean a delicate paw or two. Soon, wobbly hindquarters notwithstanding, she'd jump onto the sofa and curl against one masculine thigh. That would bring rattling of the newspaper and readjusting of arms and hands so as not to "touch the dirty thing." After another carefully-considered interval, Coal Dust would climb ever so gingerly into that one forbidden lap. Grumbling, the lap's owner would put her down. (This action was done with amazing gentleness, considering the never-say-die hostility which powered the hands.) She'd work her way back up to the coveted in-lap position. He'd put her down. She'd be back up in short order. He'd put her down. Still—up she'd go, only to be put down yet again. Still again she'd succeed in getting to her goal.

Eventually, the stronger will won out, and that was the end of the matter: from that time onward, whenever Bob provided a lap, Coal

Dust provided a lap warmer. There she'd curl, looking decidedly blissful under the double boon of warm lap beneath and gentle stroking above. The masculine rationale for the Manxish victory? "You just can't help liking *this* cat. She's so *lovable*."

Coal Dust's physical problems were obviously degenerative; when they reached the point of serious debilitation, we had to take her to the local animal shelter to be put to sleep. All of us agreed the trip was necessary and kind—but the head of the house didn't have the heart to act as chauffeur. That was understandable, really, considering the fact that said heart had been irrevocably lost weeks before to a small, furry invader.

Ah yes—the Manx's ministry to me? Simply put, it was a lesson—a great lesson—in *lovableness*. The Lord has often borne in upon me the fact that His outstanding command for Christian husbands is to love their wives; yet, knowing that full well, we wives make ourselves about as easy to love as wounded tigers. My human wisdom was soundly humbled by that of the feminine feline. There were several aspects of her conduct which stood out: she was warm—with her affection clearly evident in her actions. She was also undaunted by her man's discouraging actions and reactions. Moreover, she made that man the focal point of her attentive efforts; she concentrated wholeheartedly upon him, taking advantage of every opportunity to be near him. And finally, her delight in his attention and presence was unmistakable.

Coal Dust's stay with us was really very brief if measured by days and weeks; but if measured by *effectiveness,* it was long indeed. In fact, I doubt that there will ever be a time when my marital spirit cannot benefit from some *manifestations of the Manx.*

25
A Missing String

How do things "wind down" at your house just prior to the children's bedtime? In our home, you never know what random activities are going to be pursued as the children carry on their highly individualistic and peculiar routines of "getting ready for bed." On a recent evening, Bobby came up with an impromptu music recital.

There I was, sitting in our bedroom, physically relaxed in the certainty that the kids were indeed making progress toward retirement. Then Bobby disproved my theory by walking into the room with an appearance and attitude that didn't say "bedtime" at all. He held something I'd not seen for a long time: a castaway ukulele. Maybe "castaway" isn't the right word. The uke had been put aside ever so long ago, and it had apparently lain forgotten for months in an out-of-the-way spot (very likely under one of the boys' beds). But now, at a wholly unlikely juncture, had come its rediscovery.

Bobby was immensely pleased with his find; he was wiping the dust from the surface, blowing dust out of the body, bewailing the broken string, tightening and caressing the remaining strings. He accommodated his considerable young length into a contortionist position on the edge of our bed while continuing to handle the battered ukulele. Realizing his endeavor did not demand my concentration, I went back to writing. Before long, though, Bobby again broke into my mental pursuits with "Hey, Mom, listen to this!" He rose dramatically from the bed, struck a pose, and plunked out a brief but familiar phrase: "Jesus loves me, this I know. ..." That's all the farther it went, due to the state of the equipment. But the musician was grinning from ear to ear as he proclaimed, "See—even an old klunker with only three strings can make music!"

Well, Bobby did eventually get to bed, as did our other two offspring. Evidently the pathetic old ukulele was put back in its dusty resting place. But as the children—at last—slept, a phrase remained very much awake: "even an old klunker with only three strings can make music!"

An old klunker with only three strings. I didn't know whether to laugh or to cry as the truth gripped me: that ukulele is much like me as a Christian woman! Indeed, I feel strong kinship with that dust-laden instrument in several ways. First, I certainly don't *look* promising as a prospect for playing the music of a Christian testimony. In fact, I'm most *unlikely*. Surely anyone knowing the real me would quickly pass on in favor of someone with more brain, less emotionalism, more talent, more proven performance under pressure, more of *everything* in the way of character and spiritual equipment.

And how about the "number of strings"? Compared to many other Christian women, I'm deficient there, too. A considerable list of such women comes to mind as those who have all the "strings" in place as far as favorable circumstances go. Or material possessions. Again, a goodly number enjoy that economic level which would effectively free them for Christian service. Why, just *think* of the important strings I'm missing! The string of personality: surely I need that strong bass note of extroverted, gregarious, relaxed personality to play a really effective melody. And the string of public ease: that slender, carefully strung, high-pitched string is so effective in drawing attention to that which is said or done. Hmm. When you really consider the matter, there are a lot more strings missing than are in place on this dust-burdened instrument! Surely then, Lord, you mean for me only to sit mute in my comfortably shadowed corner and let someone else carry on the business of giving forth the music of testimony!

And yet ... there's the picture of Bobby strumming happily—and producing a phrase of music, howbeit basic, proclaiming, "Jesus loves me, this I know...." That's really utmost simplicity isn't it? Then why try to make it hard? We assign so many flourishes to "testimony" or "ministry" that the rendition demands a master instrument. But that's not what God says at all. He decimates all the unnecessary musical ginger-bread by saying, "I made you exactly the way I wanted you to be" (Psalm 139:16). "Don't look at the instrument—just give it to Me" (Romans 12:1). "I'll play the melody *I* want on that instrument, and it will bring glory to my name" (I Peter 2:9, 10).

Oh, do pick us Christian women up out of the dusty corners where we're hiding, Lord; dust us off; tighten and tune whatever strings we have; play a simple, sweet melody of praise to Your dear Self!